Based on the "Winnie the Pooh" works by A.A. Milne and E.H. Shepard.

This edition published by Parragon in 2007
Parragon
Queen Street House
4 Queen Street
Bath, BA1 1HE, UK

Printed in China
ISBN 978-1-4054-9836-4

Disney
Winnie the Pooh

Storybook
Collection

Bath · New York · Singapore · Hong Kong · Cologne · Delhi · Melbourne

Contents

Pooh's Neighbourhood

"**I** say, it's a splendid day in the neighbourhood!" cried Owl.

"It's a nice day here, too," said Winnie the Pooh.

"That's exactly what I'm saying," said Owl. "A perfectly splendid day in the neighbourhood."

"Which neighbour wood are we talking about?" asked Pooh.

"Neighbour*hood*," said Owl. "*Our* neighbourhood – the place where we live and where all our neighbours live and are neighbourly."

"Oh," said Pooh, "it *is* a splendid day in it, isn't it?"

"Quite," said Owl. "Now I'm off for an owl's-eye view!" He flew up and circled once around Pooh's house.

"What does it look like from up there?" called Pooh.

"I can see the Hundred-Acre Wood spread out below me," said Owl. "And it's a fine place, indeed."

As Owl flew off, Pooh began to think about what it means to live in a neighbourhood, and he thought perhaps he would bring a neighbourly present to his closest neighbour, Piglet.

Pooh went inside his house and took a honeypot out of his cupboard. He tied a nice blue ribbon round it.

Then he tucked it comfortably under his arm and started down the path towards Piglet's house. But when he reached his Thoughtful Spot, which is halfway between his house and Piglet's, Pooh suddenly had a thought: I *could* take this path straight to Piglet's house. Or – I could go up the path and around the whole neighbourhood. And sooner or later the path would take me to Piglet's house, anyway.

And that's what he did.

After he had walked for a time, he came to the house where Kanga and Roo lived.

"Hello, Kanga," said Pooh. "I'm just on my way to deliver this neighbourly present to Piglet."

"But, Pooh dear, Piglet lives that way," said Kanga, pointing down the very path by which Pooh had just come.

"Yes," said Pooh, "but today I'm going the long way."

"Oh I see," said Kanga. "In that case, perhaps you should join us for a snack."

"Come on, Pooh!" cried Roo. "We're going to the picnic spot."

Pooh said he *was* feeling a bit rumbly in his tumbly, so they all went together, past the Sandy Pit Where Roo Plays, up to the picnic spot to share a little something.

Half an hour – and one picnic basket – later, Pooh thanked Kanga and Roo, tucked Piglet's honeypot back under his arm and walked down the path towards Rabbit's house.

"Hello, Rabbit!" called Pooh. "I'm on my way to Piglet's to give him this neighbourly present."

"If you're going to Piglet's house, what are you doing here?" asked Rabbit.

"I'm going the long way," said Pooh.

"More like the *wrong* way, if you ask me," said Rabbit. "But since you're here, would you mind taking these carrots to Christopher Robin? I promised he'd have them in time for lunch."

Well, at the mention of the word "lunch", Pooh noticed that his tummy was feeling just the tiniest bit rumbly again. "I'd be happy to," he said.

With the carrots under one arm and the honeypot under the other, Pooh walked along until he came to the place where the stepping-stones crossed the stream.

"One, two, three, four," he counted as he teetered from stone to stone. Eight or nine of Rabbit's friends and family heard Pooh and peeked out of their windows and doors.

Pooh shouted, "Halloo!"

Rabbit's friends and family waved.

Pooh marched across open slopes of heather and up steep banks of sandstone until at last, tired and hungry, he arrived at Christopher Robin's door.

"Oh, my carrots!" cried Christopher Robin happily. "Thank you for delivering them."

"It seemed the neighbourly thing to do," said Pooh proudly.

"Would you like to join me for lunch?" Christopher Robin asked.

And Pooh said, "Well, I really am on my way to Piglet's to bring him this present. But I don't see why I couldn't stop, just for a little while."

After lunch, and a longish snooze, Pooh was back on his way.

He walked down the path through the little pine wood and climbed over the gate into Eeyore's Gloomy Place, which was where Eeyore lived.

"Hello, Eeyore," said Pooh. "I was just on my way to Piglet's house with this neighbourly present – "

"Not coming to visit me," said Eeyore. "I didn't think so. It's been such a busy week already. Why, only four days ago Tigger bounced me on his way to the swimming hole. How many visitors can one expect, really?"

And Pooh, feeling rather bad now, offered Eeyore a nice lick of honey.

Pooh put the jar down, and Eeyore peered in. He looked back up at Pooh.

Pooh peered in. "Empty," he said.

"That's what it looked like to me," said Eeyore.

"Oh bother," said Pooh.

He walked off glumly, trying to figure out how he was going to tell Piglet about the neighbourly present Piglet was not going to get.

Pooh had almost arrived at the Place Where
the Woozle Wasn't and was deciding to take
the long path around it, just in case the woozle
was, when he saw Owl flying over.

"I've seen our whole neighbourhood today,"
Pooh told him. "But now I have no neighbourly
present left for Piglet."

"The bees have been quite busy at the old
bee tree lately," said Owl. "Perhaps you
can get a fill-up there."

"That's a good idea, Owl, but
it's such a long way," said Pooh
with a sigh.

"Come along," said Owl.
"We'll take the shortcut through the woods."

So they walked together until they came to
an open place in the middle of the forest, and in
the middle of this place was the old bee tree.
Pooh could hear a loud buzzing near the top.

Up, up, up he climbed.

"Go up higher!" called Owl. "Past the bees. To
the very top of the tree.
Now, look all
around you.
What do
you see?"

The Hundred-Acre Wood was spread out below him.

"Our neighbourhood!" cried Pooh. "Our beautiful home!"

"That's the owl's-eye view," said Owl grandly.

"Oh, I can see poor Piglet out sweeping his path," said Pooh. "Looks like he could do with some company."

Nice Place for Picnics

Sandy Pit Where Roo Plays

Pooh's House

POOH'S THOTFUL SPOT

Piglet's House

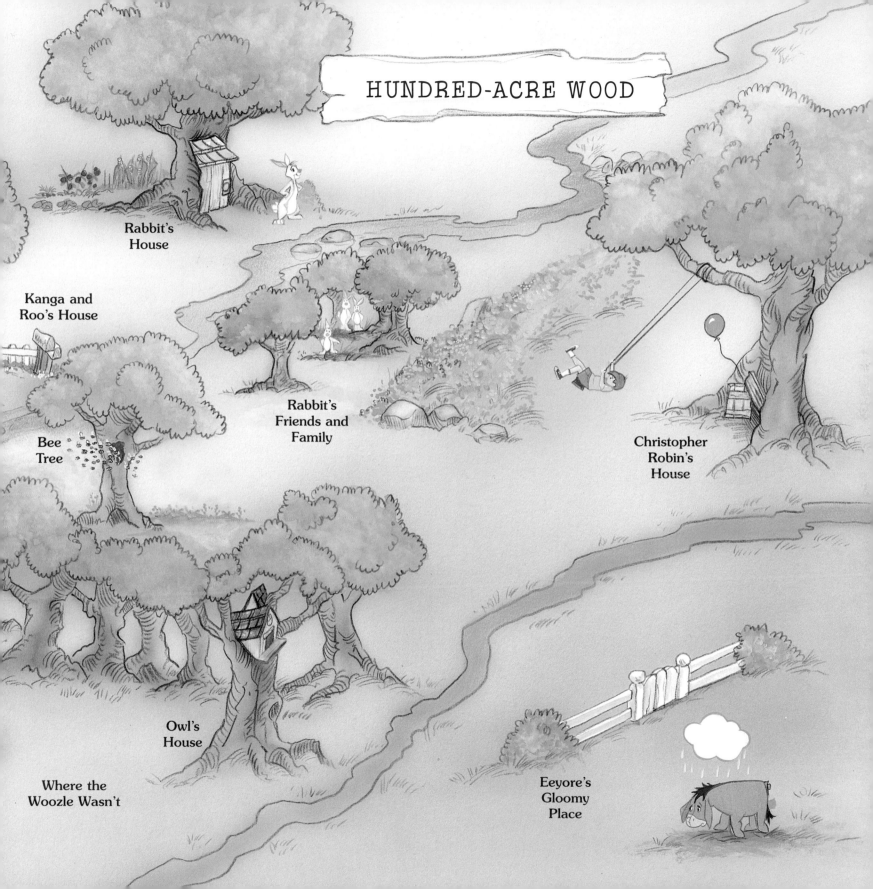

HUNDRED-ACRE WOOD

Rabbit's
House

Kanga and
Roo's House

Rabbit's
Friends and
Family

Bee
Tree

Christopher
Robin's
House

Owl's
House

Where the
Woozle Wasn't

Eeyore's
Gloomy
Place

So Pooh filled the honeypot once more, and he and Owl went to Piglet's house for supper.

Roo's New Baby-sitter

"Roo, dear, your baby-sitter will be here soon," said Kanga.

"I don't want to be baby-sitted!" cried Roo.

"Now, Roo. Mama's just going out for a little shopping and supper with Aunt Sadie," said Kanga. "You'll have fun with Pooh."

"I don't want to have fun!" cried Roo. "I'm going SHOPPING. I can shop like anything."

"Yes, dear," said Kanga. She was busy buttoning her coat and looking for her handbag.

Roo found a large bag and began filling it with things. "Look at me shopping!" he cried. "I'd be a BIG help, shopping."

"Some other time, dear," said Kanga.

"What other time?" asked Roo.

"Well, not this time," said Kanga. "Oh look! Here comes Pooh now."

"Hello, Pooh," said Roo. "I'm shopping!" He put more tins in his bag, partly because it was fun, and partly because he didn't want his mama to see how much he minded being left behind.

"Pooh," said Kanga, "don't let Roo get into any mischief."

"Oh I won't let him get into anything," said Pooh cheerfully.

"Bye-bye!" Roo and Pooh waved as they watched Kanga hop down the path and over the bridge. When she was out of sight, Roo drooped.

45

Pooh gave Roo a hug and put him
in his high chair.

"What you need is a nice smackerel
of honey to cheer you up," said Pooh.

"I want to go shopping," squeaked Roo.
"I don't want to eat."

"Hmmmm, doesn't want to eat," said Pooh.
"NOW what do I do?"

"You don't know how to baby-sit?" asked Roo.

"Well, yes," said Pooh, "all except the actual
baby-sitting part."

"I'm good at baby-sitting," said Roo. "I'll tell you how."

"The first thing a baby-sitter does is play shop," said Roo.

He showed Pooh how to set up the cash register and where to put all the toys and tins and bags.

When they had finished playing, Pooh
sat down for a little rest.

"The next thing a baby-sitter does is climb!"
cried Roo. "Let's see who can climb the highest –
you or me."

Pooh, who was beginning to think there was
not much SITTING involved
in baby-sitting, said,
"Okay, let's find a
good climbing tree."

They stood under the old apple tree in Roo's back garden. Roo jumped and jumped, but he couldn't reach even the lowest branch.

"Baby-sitters always give a boost," he said.

"I see," said Pooh.

Roo hopped from branch to branch, and Pooh climbed up behind him.

"Mmmm," said Roo. "Look at those apples. Baby-sitters always pick apples for supper."

Pooh climbed up to the highest branch. He picked four bright red apples and tucked them under his arm. Then he inched back down.

"Oh Pooh!" cried Roo. "You can climb with one arm!"

"Oops! I'm just that sort of . . ." *Thump!* ". . . baby-sitter!" shouted Pooh, as he discovered a faster way down to Roo's branch.

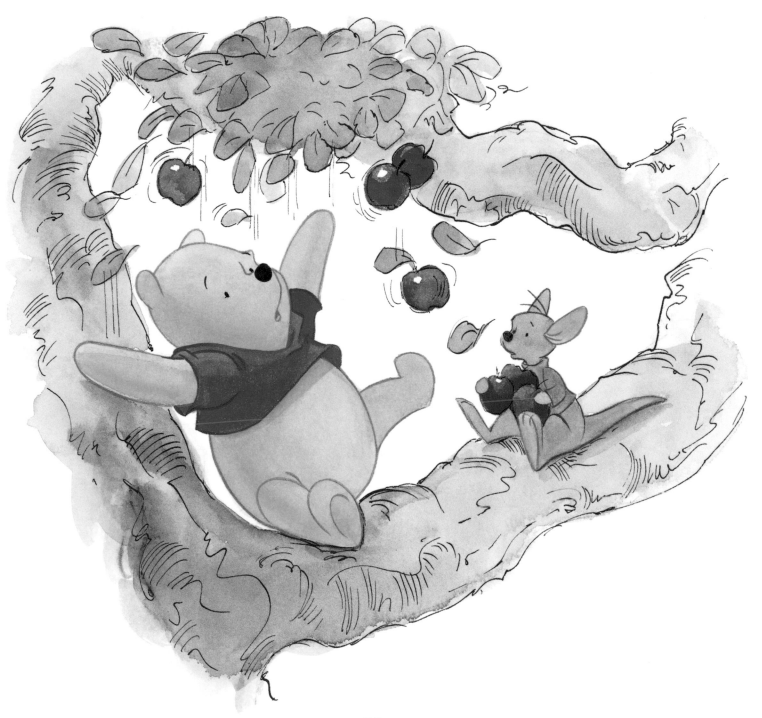

They sat side by side and swung their feet and ate the sweet apples.

"This is the best supper ever!" cried Roo.

"What do baby-sitters do AFTER supper?" asked Pooh.

"They give baths," said Roo, "with LOTS of bubbles."

Roo showed Pooh how baby-sitters pour a whole bottle of bubble bath into the bathwater.

"It seems like a lot," said Pooh.

"It's just right," said Roo.

Roo took off his little shirt and hopped in. He disappeared under the bubbles.

"Where's Roo?" asked Pooh, sort of to himself and sort of out loud. *Wfffffff*. He blew on the bubbles. He couldn't see Roo anywhere.

He swished his paws through the bubbles. He couldn't feel Roo.

"Look at me jumping," squeaked a little voice. Pooh could HEAR Roo!

"There you are!" cried Pooh.

Roo, all wet and bubbly, was jumping on his bed.

Pooh chased him with the towel and dried him off. Then Pooh helped Roo put on his pyjamas. "Time for your Strengthening Medicine," said Pooh, a little more sternly than when poohs usually say such things.

"I don't want it," said Roo. He folded his arms across his chest and stuck out his chin.

"Oh well," said Pooh, slumping in a chair. "Why don't you give ME a spoonful? I think I could do with it!"

"Now, Pooh, dear, here's your medicine," said Roo in a cheerful, grown-up sort of voice.

"Ahhh! Much better," said Pooh. "Thank you, Roo. You are a good baby-sitter."

"I'm baby-sitting!" Roo sang happily.

Kanga opened the door and saw Roo and Pooh snuggled together in the chair.

"Mama! Look at me baby-sitting!" cried Roo. "I'm baby-sitting Pooh!"

"Of course you are, dear," said Kanga.

Say Ahhh, Pooh!

"Christopher Robin says it's time for my animal checkout," said Winnie the Pooh. "He's bringing his doctor's kit to Owl's house now."

"Doctor's kit!" cried Piglet. "Oh p-p-poor P-P-Pooh – you're sick!"

"Sick?" asked Pooh. "No – I'm fine. Though I must say I am feeling a bit rumbly in my tumbly."

"That must be it, then!" exclaimed Piglet.

"What's it?" asked Pooh.

"Your tummy – it must be sick," said Piglet.

"Is it?" asked Pooh.

"Isn't it?" asked Piglet.

"Why, yes, it must be. I think," said Pooh. His tummy jiggled and jumped.

"Oh dear," said Piglet. "Let's go together. It's so much more friendly with two."

So, Pooh and Piglet climbed the ladder up to Owl's house.

"Step right in, Pooh Bear!" exclaimed Tigger, who had set up a desk near Owl's front door. "It'll be your turn to see Owl just as soon as Roo comes out."

"Christopher Robin, why do I need an animal checkout, anyway?" asked Pooh.

"Silly old bear," said Christopher Robin. "Not an *animal checkout* – an *annual checkup*. We need to make sure you are healthy and strong. And this time, Owl will give you a special injection to help keep you well."

"An injection?" asked Pooh. His tummy flopped and flipped.

"An injection!" exclaimed Piglet.

"It's okay," said Christopher Robin. "It will only hurt for a few seconds, and the medicine in the injection will keep you from getting mumps and measles and things like that."

"Bumps and weasels," whispered Pooh to Piglet. "How awful."

"Oh d-d-dear!" cried Piglet.

Just then, Roo came bouncing out of Owl's room. "I just had my checkup – it was easy!" he exclaimed. "I'll have a blue one, Tigger, please."

Tigger blew up a nice blue balloon for Roo.

"Come this way, Pooh," said Rabbit, who was being the nurse.

"G-g-good luck!" called Piglet.

Pooh walked into Owl's room, with Christopher Robin right beside him.

Once inside, Pooh and Christopher Robin were greeted by Rabbit.

"Let's sit you up here on the table, my fine young bear," said Rabbit.

Rabbit wrapped a wide band around Pooh's arm. He pumped air into the band, and it got tighter and tighter.

"How does it feel?" asked Rabbit.

"Tight," said Pooh.

"This gauge tells me your blood pressure is just right," said Rabbit.

"Now step on the scales, and we'll weigh and measure you," said Rabbit. "Aha! The perfect height for a pooh bear of your age, but a bit stout. Still, nothing a little exercise won't cure. . . ."

"I do my stoutness exercises every morning," said Pooh.

"Excellent," said Rabbit. "Keep up the good work. If you'll excuse me now, I have a great many important things to attend to. Owl will be right in."

Seconds later, Owl entered with a flourish. "Well, if it isn't Winnie the Pooh!" he exclaimed. "Splendid day for a checkup, isn't it? I say, how are you feeling?"

"A bit flippy-floppy in my tummy, actually," said Pooh.

"Hmmm," said Owl, "let's see." Owl felt Pooh's tummy. He felt around Pooh's neck and under his arms. "Everything seems to be right where it should be."

"Oh . . . good," said Pooh, giggling.

"Ah, and my otoscope is just where it should be, too – right here in my bag," said Owl.

"An *oh-do-what*?" asked Pooh.

"Nothing more than a little torch," said Owl as he peered through the otoscope. "And it will help me look in your ears . . . *mm-hmm* . . . your eyes . . . very good . . . your nose . . . excellent . . . and your mouth and throat. Open wide and say *ahhh*."

"*Ahhh*," said Pooh.

Owl pressed Pooh's tongue gently with a tongue depressor. "Wonderful!" exclaimed Owl.

Then Owl pulled a small rubber hammer from his bag. "Reflex-checking time!" he said grandly.

"What's a reflex?" asked Pooh.

"The tiniest tap on the knee, and you shall see," said Owl. Owl tapped Pooh's knee – and his leg gave a little kick.

"Oh do that again," said Pooh. "That was fun."

So Owl tapped Pooh's other knee, and that leg gave a little kick, too.

"Now, this instrument is called a stethoscope," said Owl. "It's made for listening."

"Listening to what?" asked Pooh.

"Your heartbeat," said Owl. "Would you like to hear?"

Pooh listened – *thump-bump, thump-bump, thump-bump*. It comforted him. And it didn't bother him in the least when Owl said . . .

"Sit right here on Christopher Robin's lap. It is time for your injection."

"I know it will only hurt for a moment, and it will keep me from getting bumps and weasels," Pooh said bravely.

"That's mumps and measles, Pooh," said Owl.

"Could Piglet come in and hold my paw?" asked Pooh.

"Absolutely," said Owl.

And with that, Piglet came in and sat right next to his friend, Pooh.

When Owl was done, Rabbit popped back in with a plaster. "It'll feel better before you know it," he said, patting the plaster in place.

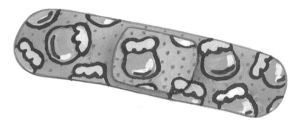

"Wow," said Piglet. "You didn't even cry!"

"An annual checkup is no problem for a brave bear like Pooh," said Christopher Robin.

I'm just that sort of bear, thought Pooh with a smile.

"Pooh," said Owl, "you are in tip-top shape, but that stomach of yours is a little rumbly. I prescribe a large pot of honey the moment you get home."

"Christopher Robin," whispered Pooh, "does that mean I can't have any more honey?"

"It means you can have a big pot of it as soon as you like," said Christopher Robin.

"I'd like it soon, then," said Pooh, whose tummy was feeling much, much better.

"T-T-F-N – Ta-Ta-For-Now!" called Tigger. "Don't forget your balloon!"

"Thank you, Tigger," said Pooh. And Pooh let Piglet hold the balloon, as they walked home together for lunch.

Tigger's Moving Day

After breakfast, Tigger stood up and stretched.
"Time for my morning bounce!" he cried. *Sproing!*
Sproing! Sproing!

"Look out!" cried Rabbit.

Thump! Tigger bumped into
one of his cupboards, and his
toys came crashing down.
"Ooooh, that happens every
time," he said with a sigh.

"Tigger, you don't have enough bouncing room in this little house," said Rabbit.

Plunk! A toy truck teetered off the shelf and landed on Tigger's head. "Ouch," he said, "it's true. But what can I do?"

"We've got to find you a bigger house," declared Rabbit. "That's all there is to it!"

"But . . ." said Tigger.

"No buts," said Rabbit. "I'm going to organize the others right away. Don't worry – we're going to find you a new home!"

By the end of the day, everyone was excited about the big new house they had found for Tigger.

103

"It IS a bouncy house," said Tigger. "The kind of house tiggers like best!" He bounced and bounced, and he didn't bump into anything.

"But," he said, sighing, "I'll miss my old house. And I won't live next door to little Roo anymore. I'll miss him, too."

"I know you'll miss being neighbours with Kanga and Roo," said Christopher Robin, "but now you'll live much closer to me. We can have fun being neighbours – just like you and Roo did."

"Do you like to bounce?" asked Tigger.

"Sometimes," said Christopher Robin.

"Besides, dear," said Kanga, "I promise to bring Roo over to visit, just as often as you like."

"Well, then," said Tigger, perking up a bit. "I hope everyone can stay awhile. We can play a game together and eat some biscuits."

Tigger looked on his kitchen shelves. There were no biscuits.

He opened his new cupboard. There were no games.

"Kind of empty, isn't it?" said Eeyore.

"Yeah," agreed Tigger. "Tiggers don't like empty houses. I like my old house better."

Rabbit put his paws on his hips and stared at Tigger. "We aren't finished yet. We need to move all your things from your old house to this house," he explained.

"Everything?" asked Tigger.

"Every last little thing," said Rabbit. "And that's a big job, so we'll start first thing tomorrow morning."

Rabbit told everyone to bring all the boxes they could find to Tigger's house. Then he told Eeyore to get his donkey cart.

"Wow! Boxes are fun!" cried Roo as he and Tigger bounced in and out of the boxes everyone brought.

"There'll be time for fun later," grumbled Rabbit. "Now we've got to pack Tigger's things."

Tigger packed all his games and his stuffed animals in a box. He took his favourite lion out and hugged him. "I want you to stay with me," he said.

Rabbit packed Tigger's dishes.

Kanga packed Tigger's hats and scarves.

Pooh and Piglet packed Tigger's food.

Soon Eeyore arrived with his donkey cart. "We can use this to haul everything," he said helpfully.

Christopher Robin and Owl hoisted Tigger's bed and table and chairs onto the cart.

Gopher loaded the boxes.

"Time to move it out!" cried Tigger.

Everyone pushed and pulled.

"Now my new home will be perfect," said Tigger, as they unloaded the cart and carried everything inside.

"Thanks for your help, everyone!" he exclaimed. "Moving was as easy as pie!"

After his friends had gone, Tigger put his toys on his new shelves.

He pushed his bed under the back window, just where he wanted it.

He set his table and chairs in the middle of the big kitchen.

He put his cereal and his extract of malt on his new kitchen shelves.

When he was all finished, he sat down to rest. Hmmm. Seems like an awfully quiet house, he thought.

He tried out a few bounces, but decided he wasn't in such a bouncy mood, after all.

"I sure miss Roo," he said.

Just then, Tigger heard a little voice cry, "Halloo!"

"Roo!" cried Tigger.

"Kanga! Come on in!"

"We've brought you a bag of biscuits," said Kanga.

"Oh yummy!" cried Tigger.

"Hallooo! Hallooo!" Tigger soon heard all his friends calling outside his new door. Everyone had brought housewarming presents for Tigger.

"Our work's all done," said Rabbit. "Now it's time for fun!"

"Hooray!" cried Tigger as he bounced from room to room with Roo. "There's plenty of room for fun – and friends – in my new house!"

Pooh Welcomes Winter

"Winter will be here soon," said Winnie the Pooh. "That's what Christopher Robin says."

"Who's Winter?" asked Piglet.

"The someone who is coming soon," said Pooh.

"Oh, a visitor!" cried Piglet. "We should do something nice for him."

"We could give him a party," said Pooh.

"What a grand idea," said Piglet.

"Come on," said Pooh. "Let's go and tell the others."

Outside, the cold wind was busy blowing the last leaves off the old oak tree. It was snowing, and the big fluffy snowflakes rushed down Pooh's collar and settled behind Piglet's ears.

"Maybe we should put on our hats and scarves," said Pooh.

Piglet rubbed his ears. "P-P-Pooh," he chattered, "p-p-perhaps we should stay at home now and tell everyone about the p-p-party tomorrow."

"But the party will be over by then," said Pooh, putting on his hat and scarf. He wrapped a Pooh-sized scarf around little Piglet twice and gave him a hat to wear.

They met Tigger along the way, and they walked to Kanga and Roo's house together. By the time they got there, they were so chilled they had to stay for tea.

When they were finally warm enough to remember why they were there, Pooh said, "Winter is coming soon, and we're giving him a party."

"Oh boy! A party!" shouted Tigger.

"Let's go!" cried Roo.

They opened the door. A pile of snow swooshed in and buried them. The wind was quiet. The Hundred-Acre Wood seemed to be napping under a thick blanket of white.

They blinked.

"How will we get to the party?" asked Piglet. "The snow's so deep!"

"Don't worry, Little Buddy," said Tigger. "We'll go by sledge!" They said goodbye to Kanga and set off.

Tigger and Pooh pulled. Piglet and Roo rode. Roo reached over the side and grabbed snow to make snowballs. Piglet piled them on the sledge.

"These will make good presents for Winter," Roo said.

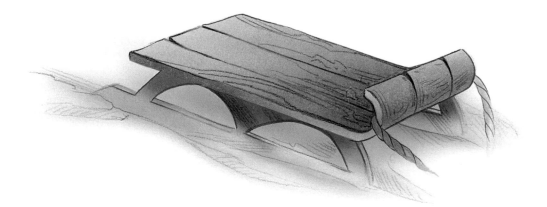

"Winter has arrived!" declared Owl, who had landed on a branch overhead. "I heard Christopher Robin say so."

"Oh!" cried Pooh. "Do you know where Winter is?"

Everyone got off the sledge and gathered round Owl.

"I haven't seen him myself," said Owl.

"We'll have to hurry and find him," said Pooh. He told Owl about the party. "Would you fly over and tell Rabbit and Gopher?"

"Don't forget Eeyore," whispered Piglet.

"And Eeyore," said Pooh.

"I'd be happy to oblige," said Owl.

As Owl flew off, Tigger and Pooh climbed onto the sledge with Piglet and Roo.

"Yaaay!" they all shouted as they slid down the hill towards Christopher Robin's house. They were planning to ask him where they could find Winter.

"There's Christopher Robin!" cried Roo.

Pooh called out, "Hallooo!"

Christopher Robin didn't answer.

"Oh no!" cried Piglet. "Maybe he's frozen in the cold!"

"That's not Christopher Robin," said Tigger. "That's Winter!"

"Winter?" whispered Pooh. "How do you know?"

"Tiggers always know Winter when they see him. That big white face – that carroty nose. Who else could he be?" said Tigger.

"Well," said Pooh, "he looks shy. We should be extra friendly." He walked right up to Winter. "How do you do?" he said. He shook Winter's stick hand. "I'm Pooh, and this is Tigger and Piglet and Roo."

Winter was very quiet.

Piglet nudged Pooh. "Tell him about the party."

"What party?" asked Pooh.

"You know," whispered Piglet. "HIS party."

"Oh yes," said Pooh. "We are so happy to have you in the Hundred-Acre Wood, we are giving a party in your honour."

Winter did not say anything.

"Oh d-d-dear," said Piglet. "He's frozen!"

"Quick!" cried Tigger. "We'd better get him to the party and warm him up."

They hoisted Winter onto the sledge.

Roo showed him the snowballs. "I made these just for you," he said.

Winter did not even look.

"Wow, he's in bad shape," said Tigger.

Tigger and Pooh pulled the sledge. Roo and Piglet pushed the sledge.

When they finally slid up to Pooh's house, the others were already there. Owl had hung a big friendly sign over Pooh's door – WELCOME WINTER. Eeyore had stuck a pine branch in the snow. Little icicles sparkled on its needles. Rabbit and Gopher were inside, making hot cocoa and honey carrot cake.

Pooh and Tigger wrestled Winter off the sledge.

"Give him the comfy chair by the fire!" ordered Rabbit. "Gopher, get him some hot cocoa!"

Everyone fussed over Winter. Still, he did not say a word. His carrot nose drooped. His stick hands fell.

"Oh my!" cried Piglet.

"Maybe he's not the party type," said Eeyore.

"Our cocoa'sss making him sssick," whistled Gopher.

"What are we going to do?" asked Rabbit.

Just then, Christopher Robin tramped up to the door in his big boots.

"Has anyone seen my snowman?" he asked.

"No," said Pooh glumly, "but maybe you can help us. We brought Winter here for a special party, but he doesn't seem to like it."

"Silly old bear!" Christopher Robin laughed. "Winter is not a who – it's a what."

"What?" asked Pooh.

"This is my snowman," said Christopher Robin.

"He's not Winter?" asked Pooh.

"No," said Christopher Robin. "Winter is a season – you know, a time of the year. Cold snow and mistletoe . . . warm fires and good friends. . . ."

Pooh scratched his nose thoughtfully. "Yes, I see now," he said. "Of course, I am a bear of very little brain."

"You're the best bear in all the world," said Christopher Robin. "Come on, we'd better get the snowman back outside before he melts completely."

"Oh d-d-dear," said Piglet. "I hope we haven't ruined him."

"Snowmen are easy to fix," said Christopher Robin. They undrooped the snowman's nose and stuck his stick hands back in.

Eeyore laid the pine branch in his hands. "Well, so much for the party," he said.

"Yes," said Pooh. "Too bad."

"Pooh," said Christopher Robin, "we can still have a party to celebrate winter. It's a great idea!"

"It is?" asked Pooh.

"Sure," said Christopher Robin. "Let's have fun!"

So everyone threw Roo's snowballs. They took turns riding on Tigger's sledge. They made snow angels. They caught snowflakes on their tongues. And they sang songs and danced around the snowman until they couldn't dance any more.

"Everyone inside for honey carrot cake and hot cocoa!" called Rabbit. They all gathered around the fire. But this time, they left the snowman outside where he belonged.

Christopher Robin gave Pooh a little hug. "Happy winter, Pooh," he said.

"Happy winter!" cried Pooh.

The End